Rosa M. Curto

# Draw the Magic Fairy

# Draw the Magic Green Fairy

**Enslow Elementary**

an imprint of

**Enslow Publishers, Inc.**

40 Industrial Road
Box 398
Berkeley Heights, NJ 07922
USA

http://www.enslow.com

# Sweet Ice Cream

2

Do you like ice cream?
You can draw ice cream treats in three steps.

If you go to a fairy party in the summer, you will find all flavors of ice cream.

3

Here are six different types of ice cream, but there are many more special flavors fairies enjoy. Other favorites are orange, walnut, honey, melon, and cinnamon.

# Little Jars

The green fairy keeps many different things inside very pretty jars.
There are raspberries, orange slices, rosemary, chestnuts, clover, and honey.
The green fairy likes honey in her tea.

4

The green fairy also makes different flavored jams and marmalades.
There are different fruits in different seasons.

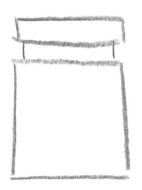   

Can you imagine what delicious breakfasts
the fairies must have?

 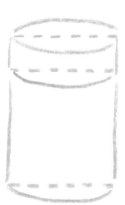 

The fairies love to make jams all year-round.

 # Baskets

The fairies weave baskets from river
reeds and wicker.

1 Draw a trapezoid.

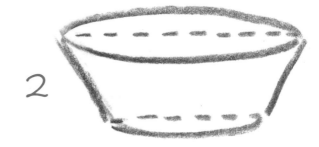

2 Round off the top and bottom.

6

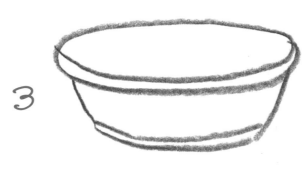

3 Outline the borders.

4 Draw some handles.

Add some color and fill the
basket with fruit.

5

The baskets are used to carry fruit, flowers, and sweet-smelling plants. Follow the six steps carefully to draw this basket.

**1**

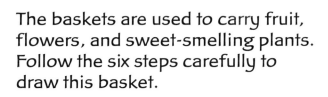

**2**

Draw a rectangle and round off the top and bottom.

**3**

**4**

Draw the handle and borders.

**5**

**7**

**6**

Fill it with what you like.

Now you are ready to create your own basket!

# Nuts From the Forest

Delicious desserts are made with nuts.

*Add nuts to ice cream and cake.*

Nuts are very good for you. That is why fairies
always have some stored away.

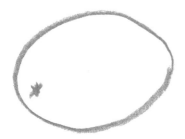  

9

The green fairy gathers enough nuts
to share with her friends.

# Vegetables From the Garden

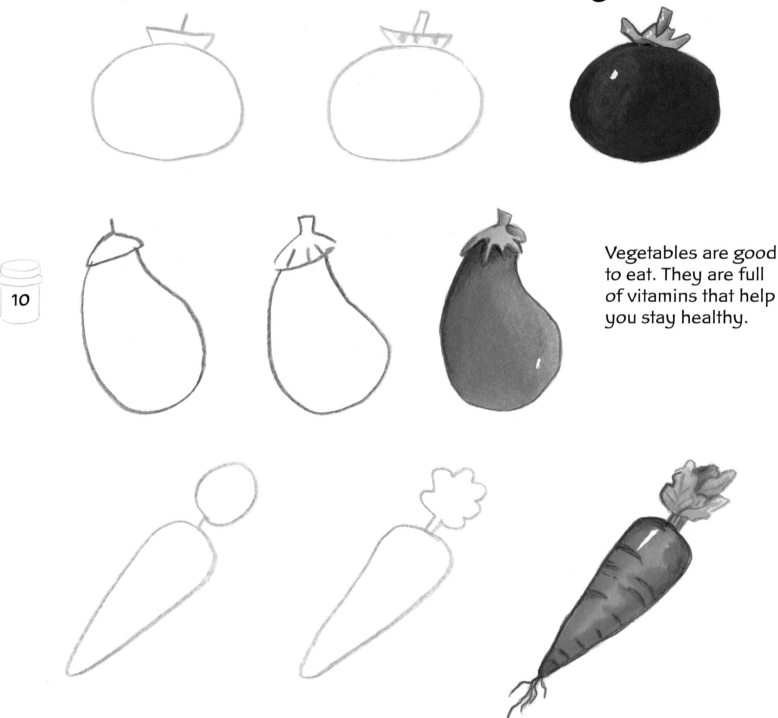

Vegetables are good to eat. They are full of vitamins that help you stay healthy.

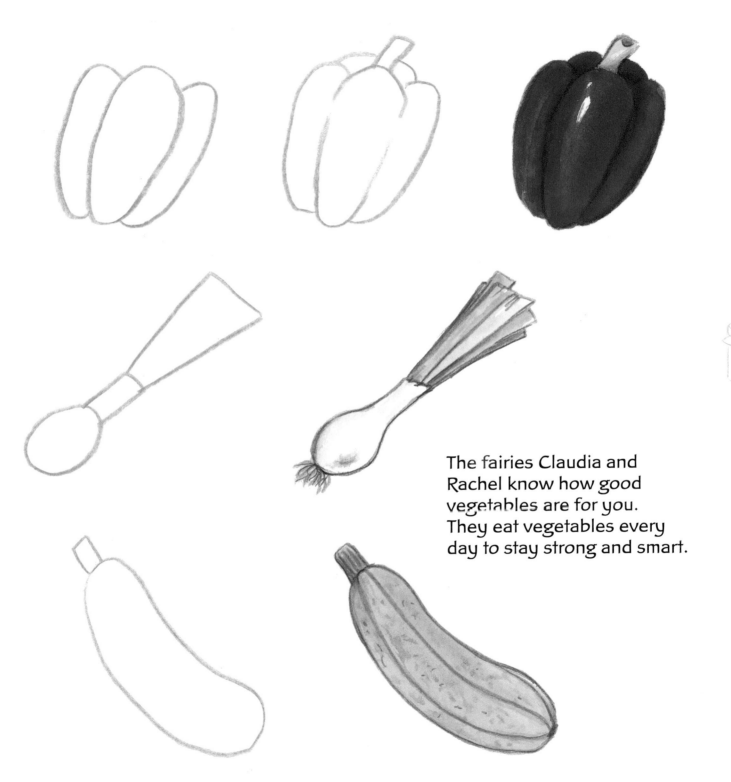

The fairies Claudia and Rachel know how good vegetables are for you. They eat vegetables every day to stay strong and smart.

# Plants Fairies Like

## calendula
### (kuh-len-juh-luh)

The forest is full of plants. The green fairy makes soap from this plant.

## chamomile
### (kam-uh-meel)

The green fairy uses many parts of the plant to make tea. She uses flowers, leaves, stalks, and roots.

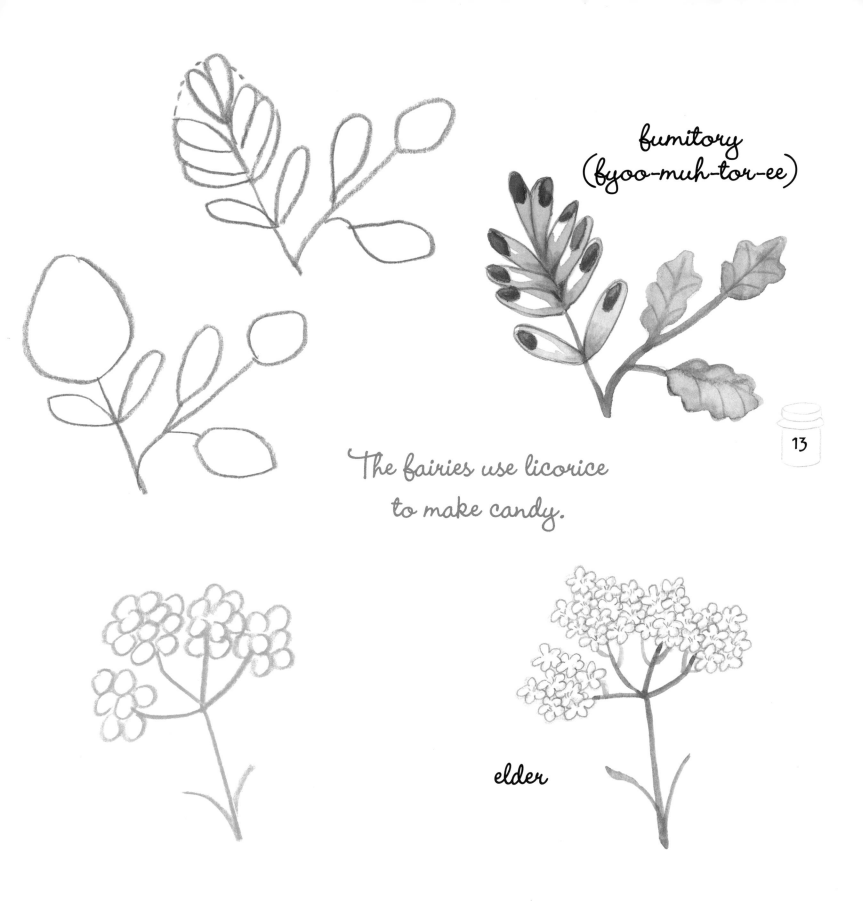

fumitory
(fyoo-muh-tor-ee)

13

The fairies use licorice
to make candy.

elder

# Buzzing Bees

14

Bees are very helpful because
they make honey and wax.

Here are eight different drawings of bees.
You can draw many bees and make a hive.

Now draw another much larger bee. It will be the queen bee.

# Ants and Other Insects

Learn to draw
a fly and a wasp
in just three steps.

16

Now draw a grasshopper
in four steps.

1

2

3

Join a circle and a rectangle together.

Draw lines on the body as shown
in the drawings.

Draw antennae, an eye, and six legs.
Add some color to finish your grasshopper.

4

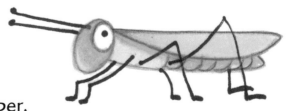

Insects are important to the fairies.

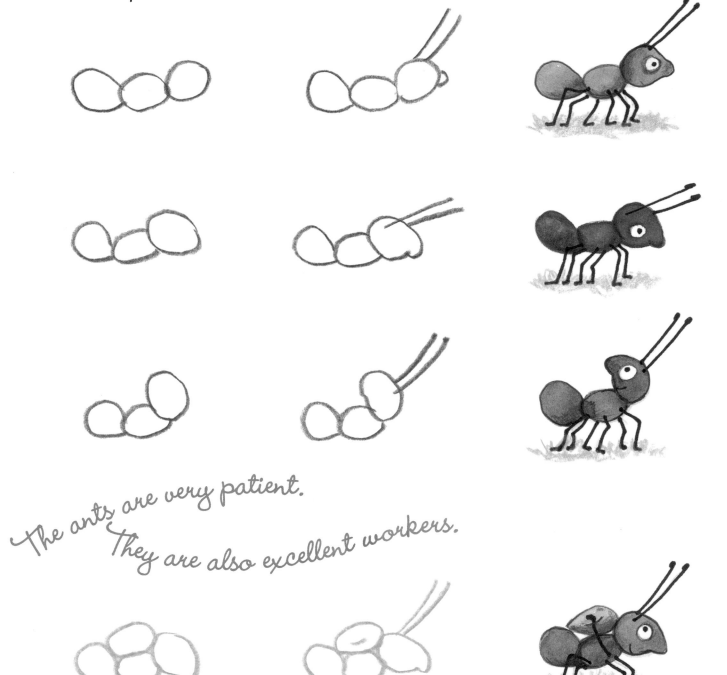

The ants are very patient.
They are also excellent workers.

17

# Mikey the Mole

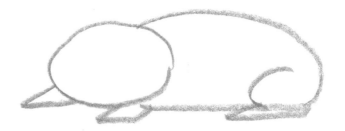

18

Now you can draw Mikey the mole.
Just follow these three steps.

Moles spend most of the time living underground.

They are very quiet. They know all the secrets
and mysteries of the forest.

# Crowns, Stockings, and Hats

Crowns made of leaves

stars

and flowers.

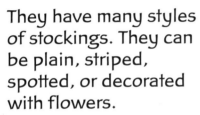

The fairies love to dress up!

They have many styles of stockings. They can be plain, striped, spotted, or decorated with flowers.

How did they make these hats?
Look closely at the flower and fruit shapes.
Draw a different hat.

# Wings

petal

Fairies can change size, and sometimes they hide their wings. They can make themselves completely invisible!

wing

wing

wing

fresh leaf

dry leaf

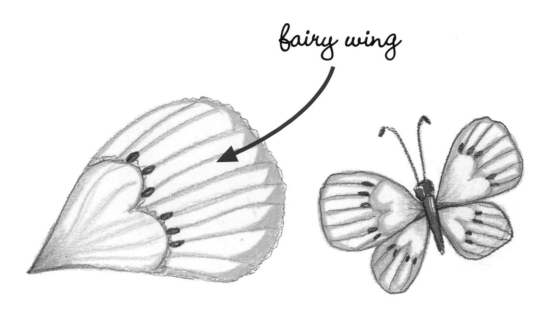

fairy wing

Fairies can blend in with the flowers, leaves, and insects.

Their wings look like dried leaves in autumn or green leaves in spring.

Fairies also have butterfly or dragonfly wings.

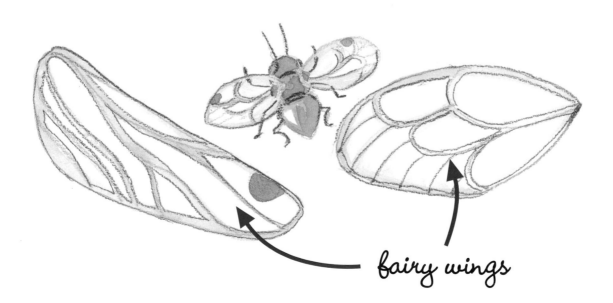

fairy wings

**1**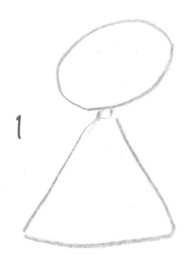

**2**

Draw a circle and a triangle.

Outline the hair and the sleeves.

**3**

**4**

Add details to the hair and the dress.

Draw the wings.

24

Mark the arms
and legs.

5

6

25

Finish the arms and the legs.

Finish the details and
paint her!

7

This fairy gathers
all the feathers she finds
so she can stuff cushions.

# The Green Fairy

**1** Draw two simple shapes.

**2** Draw the sleeves.

26

**3** Draw the waist.

**4** Add more details to the dress.

**5** Draw the wings.

6

Outline the arms and the legs.

Draw the hair and finish the arms and legs.

7

Paint her!

27

The green fairy and many of her friends are excellent dancers. All their movements match up perfectly.

8

Those who do not dance sing or play an instrument.

# Fairy Suzy

Draw two simple shapes.

1

Outline the hairline and collar.

2

3

Draw the hair, arms, and hands.

4

Draw the sleeves and the wings.

Mark the the legs.

5

Finish the legs and
other details.

6

29

7

Paint her!

Fairy Suzy is
the sweetest of all.

The other fairies

love her very much.

# Fairy Claudia

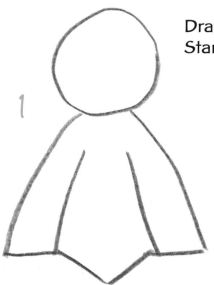

Draw a circle to make the head. Start drawing the dress.

1

2

Mark the places where the hat, neck, and dress will go.

3

Add details to the head and dress.

4

Draw the wings.

Mark the places where the arms
and legs will *go*.

Finish the arms
and legs.

Finish the details
and paint her!

5

6

7

31

Claudia is very
hard-working.
She always helps
her friends.

The fairies are very good friends with the stars and love the nighttime.

# A Starry Night

# Try to draw or paint a sky full of stars!

33

You can make several stars with
white paint on a blue background.
The smallest stars are just different
sized little balls. These stars are far
off in the distance.

# Musical Instruments

*The fairies cannot imagine a party without music.*

Their instruments are filled with seeds and stones from the forest. The fairies shake their instruments to make noise.

34

maracas

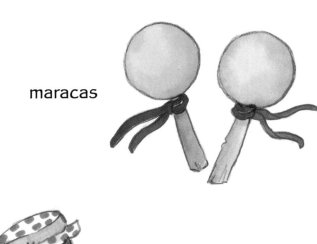

a tube
containing
rice or sand

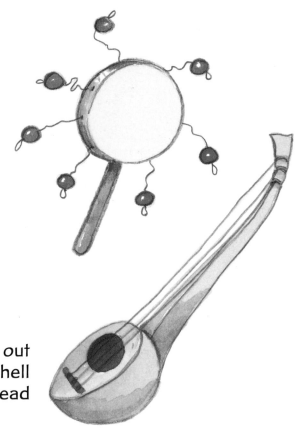

a mandolin made out
of a coconut shell
and silk thread

The fairies also make their instruments from branches, pieces of wood, stones, nuts, and flowers. You can make some instruments, too, using containers, cardboard boxes, cereal boxes, and cans. Place some rice inside a container or box. Tape it closed so the rice does not come out when you shake it.

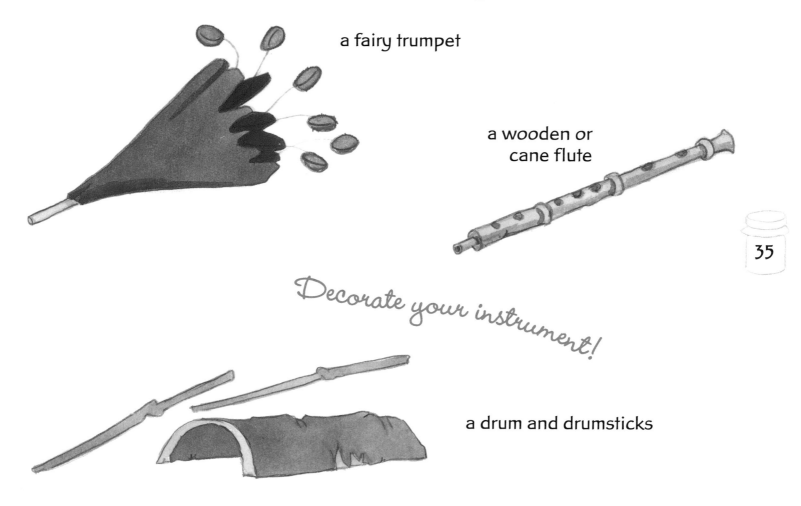

a fairy trumpet

a wooden or
cane flute

Decorate your instrument!

a drum and drumsticks

Tap the drum lightly with two drumsticks. Use different materials, such as wood, plastic, and metal. Listen to the sounds. You will hear how they change.

Let's go!

Enslow Elementary, an imprint of Enslow Publishers, Inc.
Enslow Elementary® is a registered trademark of Enslow Publishers, Inc.

Original title of the book in Catalan: *DIBUIXANT EL MÓN DE LES FADES 4*
Copyright © GEMSER PUBLICATIONS, S.L., 2012
C/ Castell, 38; Teià (08329) Barcelona, Spain (World Rights)
Tel: 93 540 13 53
E-mail: info@mercedesros.com
Web site: http://www.mercedesros.com
Author and illustrator: Rosa Maria Curto

**Library of Congress Cataloging-in-Publication Data**

Curto, Rosa Maria.
  [Dibuixant el món de les fades. 4. English]
  Draw the magic green fairy / Rosa M. Curto.
      pages cm — (Draw the magic fairy)
  Summary: "Learn how to draw the world of the green fairy, including her other fairy friends, different animals, food, plants, accessories, and much more"—Provided by publisher.
  ISBN 978-0-7660-4268-1
  1. Drawing—Technique—Juvenile literature. 2. Fairies in art—Juvenile literature. I. Title.
  NC655.C87413 2013
  741.2—dc23
                    2012030438

Future edition:
Paperback ISBN 978-1-4644-0479-5

Printed in China
122012 Leo Paper Group, Heshan City, Guangdong, China
10 9 8 7 6 5 4 3 2 1